T0197325

Greatness

Identifying, Discovering, Cultivating, and
Unleashing the Seeds of Greatness Within You

Allen Dotson

WESTBOW
P R E S S®
A DIVISION OF THOMAS NELSON
& ZONDERVAN

WestBow Press books may be ordered through booksellers or by contacting:

WestBow Press
A Division of Thomas Nelson & Zondervan
1663 Liberty Drive
Bloomington, IN 47403
www.westbowpress.com
844-714-3454

ISBN: 978-1-6642-2516-9 (sc)
ISBN: 978-1-6642-2515-2 (e)

Library of Congress Control Number: 2021903698

Print information available on the last page.

WestBow Press rev. date: 03/03/2021

THIS BOOK IS DEDICATED TO

My late earthly dad, Joe Lewis (Boy) Dotson.

My leader, motivator, encourager, and educator. What a wonderful man with a huge heart, willing to put others before himself. Outstanding work ethic. Thanks so much, Dad!

My late mother, Shirley Ann (Cole) Dotson.

One of the kindest and gentlest persons I ever met and knew. You may be thinking, *Of course you would say that. She's your mother.* Yes, she was my mother, and she was actually kind and gentle. She tirelessly gave of herself, time, talents, gifts, and resources for the greater good of other people.

And my late baby brother, Tozz (T-Bone) Dotson.

We love you, brother, always. We, your other siblings, will never forget the youngest of nine children, who was killed in an automobile accident. A brother, father, an artist, barber, and college student. Love you always!

To my remaining brothers and sisters—friends as well—love from the heart. Thanks for being my siblings and friends. Each of you mean so much to me and just how far God has brought me, us. Again, thank you for all your love and support.

Family and people going forward undiscovered gifts, talents, and abilities are just a waste of potential that could have changed so many lives. Before you throw it away or neglect what is inside of you, what you have been given, understand it is valuable. Talk about it with a professional or confidant. Honestly, it's worth discovery. When an expert wants or desires to pinpoint a thing and get it's true meaning, that person launches what is called discovery. And that's what you should do once you complete this book. Start taking steps for your own discovery now.

You may not be an expert, but you are a human being with unimaginable talents, gifts, and abilities, and they are worth your investment in them—your time—now. Wherever that leads you, it is worth it.

CONTENTS

INTRODUCTION

Greatness: The quality or state of being great (as in size, skill, achievement, or power). "Greatness." *Merriam-Webster.com Dictionary.* https://www.merriam-webster.com/dictionary/greatness. (Accessed September 16, 2020)

Many people have walked this earth. In 2019, as I write this book, the population stands at or around 7.7 billion as of 2019. (For further study, visit the link at the end of this book.) But we may never know the exact number. There are countless people walking around every day who have not identified their greatness and put it to good use. If you are one of them, hopefully this book will help you to do so. Everyone needs to start somewhere, right? Hopefully, you concur.

Depending on your age group, some of the people I'm about to mention may not be familiar to you. However, with a quick click on Google, you can find out more about their life stories. These people are real. Each of them walked this earth and discovered their individual greatness. And as they say, "The rest is history."

Some Examples of Greatness Discovered

Michael Jeffery Jordan

Some say he's the greatest player to ever hold a basketball. Now you may or may not agree that Michael is the greatest ever, but you would agree that his greatness was on display for all to witness. Once cut by his high school basketball coach, Michael did not allow that to stop him why? Because he knew better than anyone the seeds of greatness, were there on the inside of him, and all he needed to do was identify, discover, cultivate, and then unleash them. After that rejection from his high school coach Michael kept driving/moving to cultivate that greatness. Made it onto the university of North Carolina Basketball team, and as a sophomore, he, yes Michael made the winning shot/basket against Georgetown university; that cause N. Carolina to win the NCAA basketball championship. O' Michael was just getting started. After getting drafted, by one of the worst teams in the N.B.A at the time (Chicago Bulls), Michael greatness will rise to another level unprecedented. Michael would go on to help this one-time rag tag franchise, win not one, not two but 6 N.B.A championships. Mighty impressive. Just to show you that, that greatness never leaves you and is worth you discovering it. Michael is still winning with that greatness off the court as well. You have your own greatness inside of you. Go discover it.

Dale Earnhardt Jr.

One of NASCAR's beloved stock car drivers, this son of a NASCAR legend, at the time of this book Dale jr. won over 26 races in his racing career, still competes part time. Maybe there is more to come but his greatness is still on the inside wanting to be unleashed again.

Jack Nicklaus

Who does not know this guy? When you mention golf, Jack Nicklaus will always be somewhere in the conversation. The winner of seventeen professional tournaments. No person as of, yet, has won as many green jackets (winner of the Master's tournament), than Jack; Jack has won a total of 6 green jacket, he is just amazing. He has greatness.

John McEnroe

One of tennis's great players, he is also known as having a bit of an attitude, though he eased up later in life. John's play on the court in his prime was rarely matched by any competitor.

Serena William's

an American tennis player, some pundits say she is the best who have ever done it, I am not sure about that however, what I am sure about is this, Serena at an early age discovered, as she grew, identified, cultivated, and unleashed that greatness on the inside of her. Serena is the winner of 23 major single tournaments, 19 major titles, grand slam tournaments. There is no denying that Serena's greatness is on display for all to see.

Natali Portman,

Actress has played in a number of movies, one of her most noticeable rolls she played as Padme' Amidala in the Star Wars Episode 111, "Revenge of The Sith". Natali also directs films as well. Just another example of someone who discover, identified, cultivated, and unleashed their greatness for the greater good of humanity.

Michael Jackson

Singer, songwriter, and dancer, Michael traveled the world. His greatness was seen by millions. And though he's not here on earth, his greatness is still among us through his work.

Newcomers

Tyler Perry

Here's a guy who was once homeless but had the gift to make people laugh. Now Tyler makes movies and television shows. Maybe you heard of his *Medea* films. And there are so many others.

Ask yourself, "What do all these individuals have in common?" What would be your answer? Yes, there is/was one thing each did better or on a higher level than others. They all identified the seeds of greatness within them.

Some of them discovered these seeds earlier than others. Nonetheless, these individuals identified, cultivated, and unleased their greatness into society, making it a better place.

There is another thing they all have in common—a strong work ethic. You will not achieve your full potential being lazy. You must work hard.

Your greatness is *not* about being recognized, applauded, or in how many trophies you are awarded. Those things are okay in their proper places. However, your greatness is bigger than just you. Your greatness is given to you to bring change to your surroundings as well as to yourself and your family.

You were born with seeds of greatness already planted into your DNA. And they need to be discovered by you. From this day forward, do the things that support your greatness. Do not waste your time on things or people that do not benefit your greatness. Time is of the essence. Believe that.

CHAPTER 1

Seeds

What has time taught us about seeds? Seeds reproduce within themselves. Seeds need certain things to allow them to produce or perform what they were meant to do. Seeds that are planted, given the right amount of nutrients, and the proper soil and location will grow and multiply over time. Multiplication comes quicker in some areas than it does in others.

Let's talk a moment about nutrients. What are they? Nutrients give energy and allow things to develop fully naturally.

Earth, soil, is a place or destination. So is your greatness. It is designed for a particular place. You will know this place once you unleash your gifts, talents, and abilities. You will flourish at your strongest capacity at the correct time and in the correct location.

The sun is heat and, for your greatness, is probably the most important element of all. Heat on your gift will bring the best results. Heat means seasons of trouble; some seasons may be light, while others may be intense. Whatever you do, don't try to avoid or remove yourself from the heat or times of trouble. Trouble will mature the seeds of greatness that are in you. At the moment, the seeds in you are immature, and they need strength and development. Without heat, our gifts, abilities, and talents will stay as is—dull, unable, and unqualified.

Let's look at gold and the refining process. Gold's value on the surface is hidden until you apply some heat (fire) several times at different degrees. Yes, you must remove the impurities— imperfections or hindrances—from its true value and potential. The fire will remove years, and in some cases decades, of dirt and mold. And once the fire does its work, the product will be valuable and quite usable. Your greatness is like gold that's hidden. Once it's discovered, it needs heat—in this case, haters, disappointment, jealousy, and so on—to shine at its brightest. Whatever you do, do not avoid the heating process. You need it; it will benefit you. It will be difficult, but with determination, you will get through the fire and laugh about it later. And you will thank God for it.

Water is moisture. It provides a cooling of what the heat caused, allowing things to take shape and become permanent.

Care is protection from the buzzards or the enemy.

And fertilizer is for expansion and to create growth. Being around other mature people or leaders is an added benefit to your gift of greatness. Do not worry; your gift will locate and identify others.

Now let's turn toward your God-given abilities, talents, and gifts.

Every seed produces another seed of its kind, and that new seed becomes stronger than the former (its parent). Without the parent, there are no new seeds. Each seed has its own potential, its DNA, separate from its parent.

Let's get a better understanding.

I think you would agree that no two children are the same. Even brothers and sisters have their own gifts of greatness and likes and dislikes, right? If you have being paying attention to your children or grandchildren, you should have noticed differences in each of them. If not, take a closer look. Their differences are telling you that each one has his or her uniqueness or greatness. Your greatness is the same; it has its own uniqueness about itself. And your greatness will stand out. Do not try to hide it. Once you identify, discover, cultivate, and unleash your greatness, others will discover you and then many opportunities will open to exercise your greatness for the greater good of humanity, and possibly bring unto you blessings/opportunities/rewards.

CHAPTER 2

Identifying Your Seed
of Greatness

Without looking around, you probably could describe what you are wearing piece by piece. One thing we all do every day is look at ourselves. It's just something we all do. People are conscious about how they look to others and themselves.

Your greatness is identified in the same way. It is right there, just like you are looking at yourself in the mirror. Your greatness is staring back at you, asking you to unleash it.

Honestly, it is right there in your face, even though you may not recognize it. But you have exercised it and experienced it before, again maybe without recognizing it. What is that one thing you do exceptionally well, better than you do anything else in life? You excel at it, and it brings you real enjoyment. You can do other things, but with this one thing—which is your greatness—you are on another level with it. It is like being in a zone. You just flow and flow with it. Your greatness brings you joy while you exercise it. It can also be a burden to carry because of your place in society. Your greatness will be widely misunderstood by some who are close to you and by some who do not know you at all. But keep it moving forward. You've got somewhere important to go.

It is not that you are better than anyone else. There may be people who are smarter than you or more handsome or beautiful than you. But when it comes to doing that one particular thing, you stand out. Others cannot touch you. Whether you believe it or not, our Creator put a special gift, talent, or ability in you like no one else has for the good of humankind and to bring glory and honor to him.

When identifying your seed of greatness, you must embrace that one thing you do very well. When you do this, you will have identified your seed, your greatness. Remember your gifts, talents, and abilities are the areas in your life where you flow even in difficult times. Recognize them now.

Remember that your greatness is for a purpose. It solves a problem somewhere on the earth. I wrote in the "Introduction" that many people have identified their greatness and unleashed them for all the world to see and experience. Now your greatness may not bring you world attention, but it will bring you clarity, motivation, and most important, allow you to find your place in society, where you are meant to be. Someone will notice your greatness and be encouraged by it.

Even if that attention is local, your greatness will inspire change and bring hope to someone who is desperately in need of it. Your greatness will affect more people than you currently realize.

You may want to meditate on what your greatness is before going on to chapter 3. If you are sure, then move on, and let us dig deeper into your potential and greatness.

CHAPTER 3

Cultivating Your Seeds of Greatness

Now that you have identified your greatness, it needs cultivation. You do not want to put something out there that's not fully developed. If you do, it could do more harm than good. This chapter helps show you how to cultivate your greatness.

If you can, visit a farm or talk with a farmer. He or she can explain to you what really goes into growing and harvesting crops. One thing that takes place before a harvest is a season of cultivation.

If you are going to unleash your greatness, cultivating it could be the longest process. It could be the most rewarding part as well. Your greatness must develop fully in the soil before harvesting or moving on to your consumer, the people your greatness is designed to help. Every great person has gone through this process.

It is kind of like taking care of a child until he or she matures. Cultivating takes time, work, long hours, and mistakes. Yes, you will make mistakes. The farmer will tell you that some things take more of this and less of that. You will have to figure out what your greatness needs.

As mentioned earlier, the soil is the earth. It's your workplace, family, and current circle of friends. Keep in mind some may not be willing to remain your friends once you allow your greatness to come to the forefront. That is okay. It is normal.

To cultivate is to loosen or break up the soil for growing plants. It is to foster the growth of something and to improve it through labor, care, or study. It's a verb. Cultivating takes some work; the farmer doesn't just plant the seed and leave the seed all on its own. The farmer realizes that he or she must tend to the seed constantly, through all seasons of the seed's life. Why? Because the farmer is the person responsible. You are personal responsible for your greatness, so take ownership now. So be like the farmer and take ownership now.

Stir up means to set in motion. It is an adverb. The farmer also knows just what causes the seed to reach its full potential and strength. Stirring up means turning the soil. The soil allows the seed to receive the proper amount of sun exposure and moisture. Once the seed gets enough sun on one side, the farmer turns the soil to turn the seed. This gives the seed the best possible chance to become strong.

Cultivating/stirring up is also similar to cooking (depending on your age). As a kid, especially during the Thanksgiving and Christmas holidays, my mother or grandmother would be in the kitchen preparing special holiday meals. When it came time for the stuffing or dressing (whichever you call it) for the turkey or the dessert (pies especially), my mother or grandmother allowed the kids to participate. My mother or grandmother would yell into the other room, "It's time," and we knew it was time to start stirring. And one thing my sibling and I did not mind doing was the stirring for those tasty pies.

Your greatness is the same way. You must turn it, use it, even when you do not want to or feel like doing it. It is too great to stay stationary. When do you do this turning? When everything is well? No. Turn it when you have been hurt during the development stages by those you attempt to help. During times of misunderstanding sticking out like a sore thumb. Your greatness at times will challenge you to stir it up. Get up and away from hurts and disappointments, and help someone in your area of greatness. I am excited for you, at what you are about to unleash for the betterment of society and yourself. You should be excited as well about your coming potential and opportunities in life.

If you grew up on a farm, the light bulb should turn on quickly for you. However, if you did not grow up on a farm, one thing a farmer will tell you is that the cultivating process is probably the most important one of all. Why? Because this is where and how your greatness will get all the necessary ingredients to maximize its ability. In other words, just how far your greatness will take you.

As you look at your next meal, preparing to eat it, ask yourself this question: "What did this meal go through before it got on my dinner plate?" That's right, everything on it went through a process. And so does your greatness. The farmer knows the importance of turning that soil in order for the seed to survive and produce (cultivating). It takes work—hard work—and long hours. The soil could be your workplace, family, and so on. The soil, people, and atmosphere give life to your greatness and bring opportunities for you to expose the greatness inside you.

Your greatness must get into the soil. Some people will be resistant to your greatness, while others will welcome your greatness and want to see more of it. Do not be concerned about being different. I cannot stress this enough. Remember you are not better than someone else. But you better recognize you are different from others. You are destined to do what you were gifted to do. Early in your process, you may have to look for opportunities. Not forcing your way, but more like a job interview or an audition. But as you continue to cultivate your greatness, opportunities will start to seek you out. Stay humble, but release that greatness.

Once you have cultivated your greatness, you should start to notice some early signs of your greatness. How? You will come across situations that cause your greatness to surface.

CHAPTER 4

Dealing with Your Seed Killers, Haters: Identifying Your Real Enemies

You may notice I use an initial capital letter for the word "haters." I do this for emphasis. You must be aware that Haters will tempt you to abandon your greatness. Do not allow them to do so. Yes, you will have more than one, but be encouraged.

By far this is the most difficult of all the processes. If you make it through your Haters, there is no doubt that your greatness will be awesome for others to see, and you and your family will benefit from your greatness. No problem with that at all.

A Few Quick Pointers about Haters

1. Haters will hate; that's normal.
2. Haters may recognize your greatness and its potential before you do, but do not be alarmed.
3. Your greatness will expose your Haters.
4. Haters will never rise to your level of greatness.
5. You need Haters.
6. Haters will help develop your greatness.

Haters are indicators that you are on track and using your full potential of why you were born. You should shout here.

Our society has taught us the opposite of love and concern but in some places things like hate and jealousy are taught. When you have shown some success, instead of people asking how you got where you are, Haters will start hating. It's vital that you recognize these Haters early on. You may not say a word to a Hater now or ever, depending on the situation that causes your greatness to come to the forefront. But never—and I mean never—let a Hater or Haters stop you or cause you to draw back, thereby missing opportunities, or take your self-esteem away from you.

Again, you need Haters, but you do not have to tolerate them.

How to Deal with or Maneuver beyond Your Haters

It is naive for you to think that everyone who comes up to you or those who give you a pat on the back are happy for you and are your best friends. Watch out. Do not be naïve or gullible. Every person who says yes are not your friends, and to believe so is very elementary and harmful. Considering what you stand for and where you are headed, it is very dangerous to believe that each person loves you totally. Again, do not be alarmed but be aware. It is dangerous to your greatness. Please read Proverbs 17:17; 18:24 even if you do not want to. They will shed needed light on your circle of people.

So how can you distinguish who is a true friend? A friend, someone who loves and cares for you, will celebrate your greatness and not expect anything in return, though you may bless your friend with something later. When you reach your peak, your real friends will be there to help you. Your real friends are there to lift you up, encourage you when you want to quit, and celebrate you.

Very few people in your circle will understand why these celebrants are allowed to be in your circle, but you will know why. They are your real friends and your best supporters and encouragers.

When you hit a slump, and you will during the process to your greatness, your real friends will be right there and have the exact words you need at that particular time to lift you up.

That's just how important your greatness is to society. Again, read now or later Proverbs 17:17; 18:24.

Your inner circle can handle your greatness and even push you to reach your greatness in a positive way. Again, with words of encouragement as you climb to your greatness, your real friends will become even more important assets.

On the other hand, your greatness will also reveal your Haters and enemies. Do not be afraid of them, but be aware of your Haters. Remember, you need them, and your Haters cannot stop you unless you let them. Your advancement is inevitable, but it will not stop your Haters from attempting to discourage you into giving up on yourself. You must kick it into overdrive here, the gear of Determination.

Haters are the opposite of your assets, who include your real friends and supporters. Your asset will help, as I noted before, encourage, motivate, and celebrate you. Your Haters disdain you. They can neither stand you nor tolerate your greatness.

> No matter how many times your Haters smile, laugh, talk with you, and at times pat you on the back, they are not your real friends. One way you can recognize your Haters is by their camouflage—their false support of you. Using tactics like the patting you on your back, they attempt to throw you off your pursuit of greatness. You only hear from your Haters

when you are on your way to your greatness. All they want is your information. You may have gone to school with or known your Haters all your life, but they cannot stand the sight of you. They will not celebrate your greatness for even one minute. Haters try to minimize your greatness; they attempt to overshadow you or cut off your influence with others.

Again, do not be overly concerned with your Haters as they are part of life. Haters are like leeches in a swamp, sucking on your greatness because they are too afraid to go out and discover their own greatness and places in society. Haters seek to cause disturbances and discomfort for a moment. But your Haters will eventually fall off because of your greatness; here's another place to shout. You are getting close now.

CHAPTER 5

Harnessing My Gift(s)

Harnessing: To bring under conditions for effective use; gain control over for a particular end. "Harnessing." *www. dictionary. com Dictionary.* https://www.dictionary.com/dictionary/harnessing. (Accessed 5 Aug. 2020)

Another word for harness is control, and that is what your greatness needs to be for you to be able to use it best.

Harnessing Your Greatness for Its Most Effective Use

Greatness is not dissimilar to a pitcher getting a good grip on the baseball prior to throwing it over the plate. The pitcher must first grip the ball and then signal with a sign or gesture to the catcher what type of pitch is headed his way.

The grip determines the effectiveness of the pitch. Your greatness is like the process of throwing that pitch. You must harness it, bring it all together at once, release it with confidence, and watch its effectiveness once it is released.

Another Piece of the Harness Is the Belt

The purpose of a belt is to hold things in place and not letting things get out of control. Your belt (the harnessing) is vitally important to your greatness. Without a belt, things are all over the place. Being unorganized causes misuse, lack of direction, and being used by others. Please read that again! Your greatness needs a belt, a harness, an item you can trust to keep everything in their proper places and moving forward in the right direction.

Harnessing your greatness causes you to get the best and most out of your potential when needed most. Harnessing is what the elite business owners in the world call, "Working smarter not necessarily harder," making better use of what you been given. Your greatness is hard work, and once you discover it, you need to know how to put it to good use. Where it belongs.

Professionals also call this experience. You should want your greatness to go straight over the plate, meaning reaching the people your greatness is supposed to affect and change for the better. I am excited for you, and I hope you are as well.

When things are in their proper places, they serve their purposes better. Take fish for instance. Fish were made for water. A fish explodes in water; the fish's greatness comes to light. Why? Because the water is the fish's element. The water allows the fish to be and do what it was created to do. That one particular thing—swim.

Lastly, harnessing your greatness allows you, when called to do so, to release your greatness with more force and power.

Now, harness all that greatness you have been given.

CHAPTER 6

Stay Focused on Your Greatness

I am excited for you. Remember I have been through the process, and I would not have been able to write this book without the process. So embrace it. The process will benefit you and be over shortly. I am here to coach you to your finish line.

As you get closer to the fulfillment of your greatness, things may get a little hectic or confusing. People may not show respect for you. Do not worry; it is normal. All great people have encountered the same. Just do not quit; you have come too far. Your greatness will change the lives of everyone important to you, and you as well. Stay humble but determined. Speak up when needed. But you do not have to be arrogant.

Things are moving at a rapid pace now. So many things are vying for your time. It's important that you do not neglect the other important people in your life—a spouse, children, grandchildren, siblings, for example—while reaching for your greatness. Pay close attention to where you are exactly in order to achieve your greatness. It is important that you balance your time, and zero in on what is important.

You may need to adjust. You may need to add or remove items and people from your everyday routine or from your life entirely. It would not hurt you to take a moment and consult your Creator (God) through prayer "And he spake a parable unto them to this end, that men ought always to pray, and not to faint; St. Luke 18:1. "And he spake a parable unto them to this end, that men ought always to pray, and not to faint; If you are going to achieve your greatness, tough decisions will have to be made but not without counsel and guidance.

Distractions are common among achievers of greatness. There are different ways greatness deals with or overcomes distractions. For example, stay active and motivated throughout the process. Simply put, do not get bored. If you find yourself getting bored, do something. For example, read a book (an easy read), get up and stretch to stimulate your mind or move your thoughts to another subject. Take a walk or jog. These things will help you get to the finish line in one piece. Eventually the training sessions seasons will end, and it will be time to get on the field—in society full prepared—and unleash your greatness.

But before you explode on the scene, you must stay focused because distractions will come from many directions. Possibly from places you would have never thought. Even of your own making, Yes, your own doing. Avoid self-pity or bad environments. Have a core group of people you can rely on, who will pray with and for you, motivate you, and hold you accountable for your time and actions daily.

CHAPTER 7

Your Greatness Will Make Room for You

Now that you have seeds, know there's greatness in you. You have learned to identify and cultivate those seeds. You know how to deal with your greatness Haters and how to harness and stay focused on your greatness. Now it is time for some greatness to be more exposed.

First, do not run up to people and tell them what you have or can do. No, no, no. Please read the story of a young man name Joseph in Genesis chapters 37 to 50. Valuable lessons can be learned from his story.

Once you have made it this far, your greatness will open doors, maybe some old doors or new doors. Pray about each one. You may notice I mention prayer several times. It's a very good tool, and prayer can help you avoid some pitfalls the enemy—Haters—set just because they can't handle your greatness. Excitement is rising in you and rightfully so. Your greatness senses the need. Your greatness will not rest at this point. Remember to stay humble. The opportunities will present itself; be ready and not afraid.

CHAPTER 8

Putting Your Greatness to Good Use

Wow! You have come so far and through so much. You may not believe it, but you have. It may take several places, jobs, opportunities, or the correct atmosphere to find where your greatness is needed and can flourish. So do not panic if you move around a bit. Your greatness cannot be limited or squashed. Your greatness will lead you to the correct atmosphere, occupation, business, or entrepreneurship. When you get there, unleash it, let it go. Remember, your greatness is kind, not abusive or disrespectful. It is something you do better than anyone around you, and you can do it with ease and enjoyment.

Also remember Haters will be there as well. You will be misunderstood, but release your greatness anyway, without restraints. Someone in your circle needs it. You may not notice who until after you unleashed your greatness. Again, someone needs it and that is why you were born. You are accountable in a good way.

Now that your greatness is realized and growing stronger and stronger, it is more visible by others with each opportunity to its full potential. It is vital you stay levelheaded. Do not get beside yourself. Your greatness cannot be hidden any longer. Do not allow your greatness to destroy your life opportunities by becoming arrogant or hard to deal with. Your greatness brings relief and help to people and environments. In turn, you will be blessed and rewarded as well. But you must first demonstrate a trustworthiness to those higher than you, such as managers, supervisors, and so on. Remember they will notice your greatness; you do not have to point it out to them if you are ever going to soar with all that abilities you been given. People who can do things much better with ease but have a bad attitude each time they are seen will eventually get sidelined during the peak of their greatness.

But you are rising on the scene because of three things.

1. God-given opportunities
2. Levelheadedness
3. Hard work/perseverance

Allow all three to keep you grounded and levelheaded. If you do, this is what you can expect: (1) You will have success possibly for a very long time, perhaps for the duration of your life here on earth. It depends on how you handle your greatness; (2) to mentor others; and (3) leave a legacy.

It's just as easy to come down after months and years of preparation, so guard against being high-minded, thinking you are better than everyone else. You are not. You been given something great to use at a very high level. If you are honest with yourself, you know that it's beyond you, so be a good steward.

CONCLUSION

We all have potential; we were born for a good purpose. But most are not willing to invest in their potentials and greatness. You are one in a million, so go for that greatness in you. Now is the time, and time is of the essence.

I pray and hope this book, which is some of my life story, has motivated you in such a way that you are bubbling up inside with potential and are ready to bring action to discovering your own greatness. Discover it and unleash it with full confidence of a return.

Thank you for believing in yourself and your greatness. You have to believe if no one else does. Those who know me best would describe me as a compassionate man. I am a father of three sons and have four grandchildren at the time of this writing. I have a wonderful wife of more than twenty-nine years (at the time of writing this book). More on them in a moment.

I am an ordinary person who was given by God some incredible gifts (greatness). I am not a singer; I am neither an athlete nor a banker. However, I am a lover of people, all people. I have the greatness gifts of help, giving, and encouragement. I also have other gifts, but those first three stand out more than any others I possess. I can do these three in my sleep with ease and enjoyment, they come naturally, in any atmosphere now. I knew early on, around the ages of five or seven, that I was born to do something great. I was not better than anyone else was neither the smartest nor the slowest. However, my greatness just would not leave or die within me, even when I wanted to give up on it because of the pressure from people, misunderstandings, jealousies from so-called friends, and so on. My greatness just would not die. It kept springing up to the surface, no matter who tried to squash it. My greatness arose after each attack but now during an attack as well.

My greatness matched me with a grocery company in the city I live in. The company and I went back and forth for years, and I ended up spending seventeen years with this company. My greatness took me all the way to the owner's box of a $3-billion-company. Yes, I was a manager for this company. I was able to retire at the age of forty. I walked away from hundreds of thousands of dollars a year plus quarterly bonus. Pretty good at the time for someone with only a high school diploma.

My greatness has opened so, so many doors of opportunities that it would take three or four lifetimes to attempt to do them all.

I am so grateful to my Creator, God. The God of the Bible is real, Amen.

SOURCES

"Greatness." *Merriam-Webster.com Dictionary.* https://www. merriam-webster.com/dictionary/greatness. (Accessed September 16, 2020)

The current US Census Bureau world population estimate in June 2019 shows that the current global population is (https://www.census.gov/popclock/world) more than 7,577,130,400 people on earth, which far exceeds the world population of (http://www.usnews.com/opinion/blogs/robert-schlesinger/2014/12/31/us-population-2015-320-million-and-world-population-72-billion) more than 7.2 billion from 2015. Our own estimate based on UN data shows the world's population surpassing 7.7 billion.

"Cultivate." *Merriam-Webster.com Dictionary.* https://www. merriam-webster.com/dictionary/cultivate. (Accessed August 5, 2020)

"Harnessing." *www. dictionary.com Dictionary.* https://www. dictionary.com/dictionary/harnessing. (Accessed 5 Aug. 2020)

"Stir Up." *WordNet 3.0, Farlex clipart collection.* 2003–2008. Princeton University, Clipart.com, Farlex Inc. August 5, 2020. https://www.thefreedictionary.com/stir+up.

"whatsoever thy hand findeth to do, do *it* with thy might; for *there is* no work, nor device, nor knowledge, nor wisdom, in the grave, whither thou goest. (Ecclesiastes 9:10 K.J.V).

And he spake a parable unto them to this end, that men ought always to pray, and not to faint; St. Luke 18:1 K.J.V

ABOUT THE AUTHOR

The author was born into a family of 9 (6 boys and 3 girl). Raised by loving parents, who guided their children on Christian principles Allen like many others before him, got caught up in the things of the world. He knew that he did not belong there, but somehow, he GOT CAUGHT UP IN THE WORLD OF Crack Cocaine, to the point that he thought about committing suicide. Can you imagine that? But one day in 1989, he cried out to God on the side of his bed and immediately God saved him (came into his heart), Praise God! and the church was in him. HALLELUJAH!

Allen (the author) is a third generation Methodist however, he connected with a local ministry where he submitted himself to leadership, became active in the ministry because "whatsoever thy hand findeth to do, do *it* with thy might; for *there is* no work, nor device, nor knowledge, nor wisdom, in the grave, whither thou goest. (Ecclesiastes 9:10 K.J.V).

The author's faithfulness (St. Luke 16:12) allowed him to be entrusted with more responsibility and after 15 years of faithful service to his leader God LAUNCHED the author's own ministry (Miracle Center Church of Tyler). The author has gone on to have a television ministry that been airing since 2009 and still telecast each Sunday Morning Named ("Be Encourage Telecast"). The author also is the founder of an organization called Fellowship of First Christian Ministries Inc. An organization sole purpose is to aide pastors with their vision with spiritual counseling, encouragement, and financial help. God continues to favor/bless the author, he attended Liberty University (Lynchburg, Virginia), where he graduated with an A.A. in religious studies and the author is halfway through his B.S of religious studies (the author took some time off to write, to which this book was completed). At the time of the release of this book the author and his congregation (Miracle Center Church Tyler, www. mchurchoftyler.org) is preparing for a new church facility Praises only to God!!! Completion of new building late 2021 or early 2022.

The author has written several more book which will be released in the coming months, and years. A must read. "Life Lesson's/Principles Volume 1", "My Life Then and Now" "VISION What do you see?" "Doing It God's Way", "A Life Yielded to God", and

"Life Lesson's/Principles Volume 2"

All A must read.

Finally, the author been married for over 29 years to Mrs. Carolyn, My wife has been such a tremendous encourager, supported, during this entire writing period. Thanks! Baby.

and they currently have 3 sons Kendale, Joshuwa and Kerry, and 4 grandchildren and 2 on the way. Praise God!!!

The author will give up his Bishopric someday. The authors have other ventures to achieve, starting a foundation for his late Brother Toss (T-bone) Dotson, and the author desires to volunteer time to worthy none-profit organizations.

For more information on the author please visit:
www.mcchurchoftyler.org

Available Now

Greatness: Identifying, Developing, and Unleashing Your Seeds of Greatness

Coming Soon

Life Lessons/Principles, Volume 1 (November 2021)

2022

My Life Then and Now
Vision: "What Do You See?"
A Life Yielded to God

Coming 2023

Doing It God's Way
Discovering Your Own Identity in God
Life Lessons/Principles, Volume 2

Printed in the United States
By Bookmasters